Our Walk Through The World

Six Short Plays

GW00566594

Ross

A SAMUEL FRENCH ACTING EDITION

FOUNDED 1830

SAMUELFRENCH.COM
SAMUELFRENCH-LONDON.CO.UK

FOR PRODUCTION ENQUIRIES

UNITED STATES AND CANADA
Info@SamuelFrench.com
1-866-598-8449

UNITED KINGDOM AND EUROPE
Plays@SamuelFrench-London.co.uk
020-7255-4302

Each title is subject to availability from Samuel French, depending upon country of performance. Please be aware that *OUR WALK THROUGH THE WORLD* may not be licensed by Samuel French in your territory. Professional and amateur producers should contact the nearest Samuel French office or licensing partner to verify availability.

MUSIC USE NOTE

Licensees are solely responsible for obtaining formal written permission from copyright owners to use copyrighted music in the performance of this play and are strongly cautioned to do so. If no such permission is obtained by the licensee, then the licensee must use only original music that the licensee owns and controls. Licensees are solely responsible and liable for all music clearances and shall indemnify the copyright owners of the play(s) and their licensing agent, Samuel French, against any costs, expenses, losses and liabilities arising from the use of music by licensees. Please contact the appropriate music licensing authority in your territory for the rights to any incidental music.

IMPORTANT BILLING AND CREDIT REQUIREMENTS

If you have obtained performance rights to this title, please refer to your licensing agreement for important billing and credit requirements.

OUR WALK THROUGH THE WORLD was first produced by Ash Angel at The Old Red Lion Theatre on 21st October 2013. The performance was directed by Timothy Trimingham Lee, designed by Martin Thomas and stage managed by Lucy Cain with sound by Rob Hart and lighting by Matthew Swithinbank. The cast was as follows:

TILLY (AN INTRODUCTION)

TILLY. . . . . Violet Patton-Ryder

RULES OF ASSORTMENT

MIKE . . . . James Hender
HANNAH. . . . . Shani Erez
ANGELA . . . . .Joyce Springer

OUR PROSPECTS FOR THE COMING SEASON

THE MANAGER. . . . . John Atterbury
THE PROSPECT . . . . Rob Cavazos
THE AGENT . . . . Samuel John
THE PRESS PACK . . . . Shani Erez, Violet Patton-Ryder and Billie Vee

RELINQUISH

YOUNG WOMAN . . . . Billie Vee
MOTHER. . . . . .Joyce Springer
SON . . . . Joe Jameson

THE VIEWING

MOTHER. . . . . .Shani Erez
FATHER. . . . . .James Hender
ESTATE AGENT. . . . . Rob Cavazos
TOMMY. . . . . Joe Jameson

FRISKY & THE PANDA MAN

DR OGDEN . . . . Samuel John
FRISKY . . . . .Billie Vee
THE INTERVIEWER . . . . Violet Patton-Ryder

CONTENTS

TILLY (AN INTRODUCTION) p.9

RULES OF ASSORTMENT. p.15

OUR PROSPECTS FOR THE COMING SEASON p.27

RELINQUISH p.37

THE VIEWING. p.47

FRISKY & THE PANDA MAN. p.61

Please see individual plays for character and staging information.

A dash (—) after a word denotes an interruption or an inability to complete the word or sentence. An ellipsis (...) denotes a trailing off.

ACKNOWLEDGEMENTS

Edward Emanuel, Jerry L. Crawford, Terry Miller, C. Tim Quinn, Gerard Reidy, K C Davis, Len Evans, Taylor Hanes, Kelly Barnett, Jeanine Merten, Danielle Cash, Ashley Semrick DesRochers, Leslie Martin, Kendra Glazebrook, Misti Boettiger, Eric Mecum, Timothy Trimingham Lee, Dana Martin, Jane C. Walsh, Melissa Gibson, Hannah Rebecca Gamble, Jakob Holder, Luanna Priestman, Lucy Hume, Felicity Barks, Amy Rose Marsh, Casey McLain, Abbie Lucas, Sarah Norris, Chris Ryan, Amanda Berry, Veronica Lee, Sarah Girard, Mike Catterall, Hannah Gosling, Angela Stansall, Keith Osbourne, Jonny Howard, Peter Catterall, Rowan Marshall, Lawrence Cohen, Nicholas Thompson and Peter Corkhill.

For Quinn M. Corbin

Tilly (An Introduction)

CHARACTERS

TILLY – 28.

TILLY (AN INTRODUCTION)

(A light on **TILLY** *who is making a video application to be a surrogate mother.)*

TILLY. "Pick me! Pick me!" ...Nah... *(She takes a deep breath and smiles warmly.)* Well, hello about-to-be-Mummy-and-Daddy. My name's Tilly. I'm 28. I'm single. "Yay me!" *(A beat)* No, I was engaged. To a humanitarian aid worker. But when he went overseas he was captured by a vigilante terrorist group and got beheaded. He didn't survive. Obviously. War. What an enterprise! *(A beat)* We hadn't known each other that long but when something like that happens you just need a little "me time"...and nine months sounds just perfect. I don't drink, I don't smoke and I'll never have an accident or fall down the stairs at work because I don't have a job. I say it's the economy but my uncle says I'm unemployable. But he's just got sacked for eating the food from the pet shop he worked at so...people in glass houses... *(A beat)* Well, actually I do feel partly responsible for that. I was sort of seeing his manager and had recently broken things off. You just wonder if I hadn't have done that, Gary may have gone a little easier on Uncle Jim. The whole thing just seemed to smell of revenge, you know? *(A beat)* He's something. Gary. He moonlights as a taxidermist. He's into stuffing all kinds but obviously he draws mainly from what keels over in his shop. The animals that die and he can't then sell as household pets. Waste not want not, I suppose. *(Pause)* Gary. His sense of humour isn't tremendous but he's nice. And kind. More when he wants something, but still. He can be kind. He just isn't for me. *(Silence)* It was the sex really. If I can say that. If I can be in the business of honesty. *(Thinking*

11

carefully) I liked that he was a taxidermist. Well, it was interesting at first. "He stuffs dead animals". It was unique. And different. Apart from my fiancé, I've only ever had a couple of guys from the emergency services and a telemarketer. Vanilla types. But Gary… he, he was like a…a…an artist. But we could only do it upstairs, in his flat above the shop, and it was just those animals he kept up there. They're still there. Well, they just creeped me out. I mean they were everywhere. I know he has to keep them someplace, but it was…it was just…their eyes. These eyes, that I felt burning into me, following me around the room. He didn't care, but there we'd be in bed, two lonely people lying in a wet spot staring up at the ceiling, you glance over to your left or right and there's a team of mounted chinchillas staring right back at you. It's just not what you picture for yourself. When he lit candles it looked like a haunted house. The shadows and all that. *(A beat)* That flat. It's like Noah's Ark. *(A beat)* I'd tell him, about the eyes and all that and he did offer to turn them all round but of course then it'd just be hairy arses, wouldn't it? Hairy arses following you around the room. It's not ideal. *(Pause)* Anyway, I said I didn't want to see him again and I haven't, so all that's to say when I know my own mind I stick to it. I just feel bad for Uncle Jim. *(A beat)* He's in the next room. I'd ask him to come in and say hello but he's busy at the dinner table counting the sachets of sugar he collects from places. *(Silence)* Um, what else… *(She sees something.)* Oh, look. *(She gets out of her seat and picks the item off the floor and sits back down.)* 10p. *(She shows the coin to the camera and continues to hold it tightly. Pause)* I'm a big believer in talking to an unborn child, so I'll read it stories every night. I have an iPod shuffle so I can put the headphones against my belly, so it can listen to music…and I also speak a little Spanish and so I'll teach it that too. Because you know, that's a life skill: bilingual…ism. *(Brief silence)* I'd carry your baby with dignity at all times which I think is important. Some don't, do they? Not to be bitchy but it's like "Thunk. This happened. I'm doing sod all for the next nine months." No, I'd still remain active. Within reason. It's very exciting. I bet you're excited. I picture you both as lovely. Daddy, I see you as strong and gentle. You like to mountaineer and pitch tents. But just as happy sitting at home watching something on television. Maybe one of those quiet sports with gentle clapping and whispery announcers. Like golf or cricket. Or even some cheeky snooker. Mummy, you always smell beautiful and can do six things at once and are considered among your friends as "the elegant one". You also like to mountaineer. That's how you met in fact. On the face of a mountain and by the time you got to the top you were together. Your noses all runny and wearing funny hats, smiling at each other. There's a photograph above the fireplace that captures the day. Don't worry if this isn't you. This can be metaphorical. You watch Daddy watch television and picture him with a little girl on his lap. Or boy. Or both. And you think "I wonder how Tilly's getting on. Not long now!" *(A beat)* You have a lot to look forward to. My mum loved being a mum and my dad loved being a dad. They're dead. A motorway car crash one Christmas Eve. Eeek. It was bonkers. *(Thoughtfully)* We always had fun summers and we always had warm winter Sundays inside. *(Proudly)* We had a fireplace. *(A beat)* Just think of all the times you'll have together! I'm sure nothing will go wrong for you. *(Silence. She listens for something.)* Uncle Jim?... *(She listens.)* ... UNCLE JIM?! ... *(She hears something and immediately looks relieved.)* He's moving around now. Sorry. It just went a bit quiet in there. Where was I? *(Silence)* It's very exciting. I bet you're exci-oop— *(She pulls out her tongue and appears to pick something off it and looks at her fingers.)* Sorry, I bet you're— *(She pulls out her tongue again and appears to pick something off it and looks at her fingers.)* I bet you're— fuck, I've got like all kinds of hair in my mouth! Hang on. Sorry. *(She pulls out her tongue and appears to pick something off it.)* There. *(She swirls her tongue and bites to make sure.)* Three strands. Bonkers. *(A beat)* Yeah, I bet you're excited. *(Brief silence)* Imagine that day when you get to hold your baby for the first time. Unconditional love both ways starts now! Boom! *(She laughs and then stops.)* You know, I really didn't give it much thought when I had an abortion. What it'd be like to actually have a baby. It was a long time ago, I was sixteen, it was an accident and I just wasn't ready and was just scared. *(Suddenly, reassuring)* Oh I won't get another. It's not like tattoos! I mean the doctor was very nice about the whole thing really. And honest. He told me right before "This will hurt" and he was right. It did. *(A beat)* After and that. *(Silence. Then, from her very soul)* But now I would really, really, really like to have this baby. *(Silence)* And give it to you. *(A beat)* Pick me. *(A beat)* Thank you.

(She looks down at the 10 pence piece and squeezes it tightly. The light fades on **TILLY**.*)*

End of Play

Rules of Assortment

CHARACTERS

HANNAH – manager of a national bank's call and sorting centre.

ANGELA – a team leader.

MIKE – recently hired at the centre.

SCENE

HANNAH's office. On the desk are a laptop computer, the usual office stationery, a phone and a huge bowl of jelly beans.

AUTHOR'S NOTE

To be performed at breakneck speed.

RULES OF ASSORTMENT

(**HANNAH** *sits behind her desk.* **MIKE** *enters.*)

MIKE. Ms Dawson.

HANNAH. Hannah, please. You're the new...

MIKE. Mike.

HANNAH. Mr Mike. Fantastic.

MIKE. No, Mike. That's my first name.

HANNAH. Oh. Okay. How unusual. Hannah. Mike.

MIKE. Yes.

HANNAH. Well, now that we're best friends, please, take a seat.

MIKE. Thank you.

HANNAH. So how are things going for you so far? Here at the bank?

MIKE. I like it.

HANNAH. And Angela is your team leader, yes?

MIKE. That's right.

HANNAH. So what is it about the centre that you love so much?

MIKE. Oh...ahm...well. It's a good place to work. I get on well with my colleagues...I...

HANNAH. Team mates.

MIKE. What?

HANNAH. You get on well with your team mates.

MIKE. Oh right. Yes. My team mates. I think they like me and I like them. It's all been very smooth so far.

HANNAH. Good.

MIKE. Anyway, what I've come in for...what I'm concerned about is how—

HANNAH. *(gestures to the bowl of jelly beans)* Jelly bean?

MIKE. No thank you. So what I was wanting to know was, I'm a bit concerned—

HANNAH. *(as before)* Jelly bean?

(Silence)

MIKE. May I?

HANNAH. *(enthusiastically)* Go right ahead!

*(Feeling forced, **MIKE** takes a jelly bean from the bowl and pops it into his mouth. **HANNAH** picks up her telephone and hits speed dial.)*

HANNAH. *(gushing)* Angela? We've got a keeper here. He went straight for the bowl! Come in and join us... *(To **MIKE**)* What colour did you get?

MIKE. Ahm, I think it was a red one.

HANNAH. *(into the phone)* He's got a red one. He's chewing on it now.

*(**HANNAH**, elated, puts the phone down.)*

HANNAH. That's just fantastic!

MIKE. I must say, one doesn't know whether to help yourself or wait to be offered.

HANNAH. General rule is if they're closer to you, they're yours to take at any time. If they're closer to the person whose desk it is, they're not.

MIKE. Your secretary has them very close.

HANNAH. Gillian? My PA? That's her lunch. *(A beat)* No you can say it. She's hideous. Good worker though. Reliable.

MIKE. Anyway, job security is very important to me and...

*(**ANGELA** enters cheerfully.)*

ANGELA. So you got a red one? I wondered where you'd got to.

HANNAH. Angela, was this the chap you were telling me about? I really wouldn't have guessed. He seems fine.

MIKE. *(to* ANGELA*)* I'll be back there in a sec. I just wanted to find out when it is that I actually get—

ANGELA. I always tell Hannah, I say, "Watch out for the red ones. They're the chewiest." She never believes me.

HANNAH. She says it's the beeswax.

ANGELA. Now, don't go making me look stupid, Hannah. *(To* MIKE*)* I say it's the carnauba wax. They put more carnauba wax in the red ones.

HANNAH. That's for the shell! They would be harder not chewier!

ANGELA. *(playfully)* Oh stop it! *(To* MIKE*)* What do you think?

MIKE. Well, ha! I don't know. I was just trying to find out about my tax code and more importantly, when I'll get paid. You know, single parent—

HANNAH. Try an orange one.

MIKE. Really, I'm fine. It's the start of the new year. School uniforms, PE and games kits, what have you… I'm just a little worried…

(Silence. HANNAH *frowns. She looks over at* ANGELA. MIKE *notices this.)*

MIKE. Okay. Let me see.

*(*MIKE *takes an orange jelly bean from the bowl and pops it into his mouth. Both* HANNAH *and* ANGELA *lean in.)*

HANNAH. Same texture?

ANGELA. Or less chewy?

MIKE. Well, I… *(laughs nervously)* who's responsible for paying me?

ANGELA. Mike.

HANNAH. Be serious.

MIKE. Well, I can't tell.

ANGELA. Oh you will.

MIKE. They all taste the same to me.

HANNAH. You really think they taste the same?

MIKE. Well… *(turns around to look at* **ANGELA** *who is staring hard right back at him)* …I think they are…similar?

HANNAH. *(exhales, relieved)* Never "the same". Never say they're "the same". People take their jelly beans very seriously around here.

MIKE. I can see you like your jelly beans, that's for sure. *(A beat)* Okay. So I can get back to work. About getting paid.

HANNAH. *(nods like she's listening)* Hmmh. Hmmh.

MIKE. It's been a month.

HANNAH. *(nods like she's listening)* Hmmh. Hmmh.

MIKE. How does it work around here?

HANNAH. Well Mike, it's a very exciting time for all departments here. In Mortgages, they got what, Angela? Berry blue?

ANGELA. Berry blue.

MIKE. Berry blue?

HANNAH. Jelly beans. When I arrive in the morning and I walk past their desks, you can't see the paperwork for the smiles on people's faces.

ANGELA. In Credit Cards they've got strawberry daiquiri.

HANNAH. Kiwi on reception, satsuma on Estates. Just wait until you see what we're doing in Savings and Investments. Apricot isn't it, Angela?

ANGELA. Apricot.

*(**HANNAH** gestures towards the bowl and takes a jelly bean for herself which she pops into her mouth.)*

HANNAH. Grab an apricot. They're really juicy.

MIKE. No, thank you.

HANNAH. I said grab an apricot they're really juicy.

MIKE. *(standing his ground)* No. I'm fine. Thank you.

*(**HANNAH** takes a jelly bean from the bowl and places it in front of **MIKE** on the desk. They both look down at the jelly bean. They both look at each other. **HANNAH** gestures for **MIKE** to take it.)*

MIKE. *(pushing the jelly bean towards* HANNAH*)* Thank you. I'm fine.

(Pause)

MIKE. Please. All I want to know—

HANNAH. Is this what you meant, Angela?

MIKE. Meant?

ANGELA. Yes, though I have to admit I didn't think he'd do it in here as well. Not in front of you.

MIKE. What? Do what?

(Silence)

What? What am I—

HANNAH. You don't like our jelly beans?

MIKE. It's not that. I just don't want them now. *(Laughs nervously)* I've had two already.

HANNAH. *(scoffs)* Two?

ANGELA. *(amused)* Two?

MIKE. Yes. Two.

ANGELA. I thought when you called me about the red one he was up to something. He has never shown an interest in the team.

HANNAH. So it was all a game was it, Mike?

MIKE. What?

ANGELA. And he was reluctant to take the second one.

HANNAH. I offer you an apricot and you just refuse?

MIKE. Listen, all I came in here for, all I want to know is—

ANGELA. This is what's been happening ever since he got here.

MIKE. What's been happ—

ANGELA. And here he goes again. He does this a lot as well.

MIKE. What? What do I do?

ANGELA. He can be very argumentative.

MIKE. I'm not.

ANGELA. You see? It's like a red rag to a bull.

HANNAH. And this is what he's like from nine to five every single day?

ANGELA. Sometimes worse.

HANNAH. I thought you had a family, Mike.

MIKE. I do.

HANNAH. Well are you like this at home?

ANGELA. He must be.

HANNAH. At the beach, when your children are building sandcastles, do you just kick them down?

MIKE. No.

ANGELA. I don't think he's ever given up a window seat.

MIKE. I have!

ANGELA. Now he's aggressive!

HANNAH. Let me tell you something. When I first got here it was just macadamia nuts and cashews. This place was a mess. A nightmare. And productivity was low. And I mean "low".

ANGELA. Morale was terrible.

HANNAH. Morale was awful. People were weeping at the photocopier, electrocuting themselves, charging head first into the filing cabinets. Angela's partner in Mortgages even set himself on fire!

ANGELA. That's how we met. I put him out.

HANNAH. I brought in the jelly beans and not only did it brighten the place up, it got the staff going again. Rekindled the flame of enthusiasm for work. We're now the third best performing regional office for the bank in the country.

MIKE. Well yes, I've seen the annual reports.

HANNAH. You've seen them and yet you still try to undermine what we have here?

MIKE. I'm not trying to undermine anything.

HANNAH. Under my management here things have never looked so good. Beans mean growth.

ANGELA. We're thriving.

HANNAH. So what is it you're trying to do? Bring us down from the inside?

MIKE. No.

ANGELA. He denies things frequently.

HANNAH. I can see. It's the way you're going about it that troubles me. Not once in your weekly self-evaluation reports have you mentioned your disgust for the confectionery we have here. You're sneaky.

ANGELA. Not a team player.

HANNAH. And it's the teamwork that makes the dream work here at the Royal Providential Co-operative Bank.

(Silence)

MIKE. I…I don't know what to…

*(**MIKE** gestures towards the jelly bean on the desk.)*

What if I…

ANGELA. And that will make things alright, will it?

HANNAH. I don't believe you want it. I think you're just trying to save your skin.

MIKE. Are you sacking me?

HANNAH. Well, you seem to be paving that path all by yourself.

(Pause)

MIKE. But I'm a single parent. I'm good at my job. Three, four times daily I'm complimented by customers about my excellent telephone manner and my quality customer care. My data entry is accurate and I'm able to multi-task second to none.

*(**MIKE** looks to **HANNAH** who seems unmoved. **MIKE**, dejected, looks at **ANGELA** who appears rather smug. **MIKE** looks back at **HANNAH**.)*

MIKE. Can I be honest with you?

HANNAH. As long as it's not another slur on my leadership.

(Pause)

MIKE. It's not that I don't like jelly beans.

ANGELA. Oh, it's not that he doesn't like jelly beans.

HANNAH. Now, now. Let's hear what Mr Mutiny has to say.

MIKE. It's not that I don't like jelly beans. I love them. It's just...I don't believe they've been allocated as effectively as they could have been.

ANGELA. Oh come on.

HANNAH. No, Angela. Let's hear him out.

(Pause)

MIKE. With all due respect...the auras are wrong.

HANNAH. The auras?

MIKE. Uhm, yes. Well, in Estates you have the satsuma jelly beans, don't you? That's what you said.

HANNAH. That's right.

MIKE. And they're orange.

ANGELA. Sherlock Holmes.

HANNAH. Angela, shush.

MIKE. Orange is an outgoing, joyful colour. What I'd say is that if you're on Estates, dealing with people calling in who have recently lost a loved one, it might not be the best thing to have...ahm...team members...all bubbly and enthusiastic.

HANNAH. *(thoughtfully)* We have had some complaints about the Estates team sounding a little too chirpy at the news of customers' bereavements.

MIKE. There. You see? Now, green is the colour of healing and renewal. May I suggest swapping the satsuma in Estates with the kiwi on reception? Warmth and joy at reception. Understanding and consolation on Estates.

(Silence)

HANNAH. *(impressed)* That's very good.

MIKE. May I continue?

HANNAH. Please do.

ANGELA. But—

HANNAH. Shush.

MIKE. In Voucher Processing, we should have apricot. Yes. Yellow is a mental colour in the aura. Analytical skills will be at their peak. Combing through all those cheques. Well, it's a precise science.

HANNAH. Voucher Processing…apricot.

ANGELA. Hannah.

MIKE. *(on a roll)* Now the reason why Credit Cards is doing so well is because they've got strawberry daiquiri. Red can be impulsive, but it's a target driven colour. We want people to use their credit cards, we want to sell people our credit cards, we want target driven team members. But the infrastructure is already in place with strawberry daiquiri. You obviously knew that before. A woman of your renown.

HANNAH. Well, yes…I…

MIKE. Some people are just in touch with their auras without knowing it. I can see that you're one of them. It shows you have depth.

HANNAH. Thank you.

MIKE. No problem. *(A beat)* Berry blue in Mortgages was a really smart move.

HANNAH. It was?

MIKE. Blue reflects intuition. I would assume berry blue must be one of your favourites.

ANGELA. Hannah.

HANNAH. I do like them I have to admit.

MIKE. *(gestures to the bowl)* What do you have here?

HANNAH. *(almost flirtatiously)* Why, all flavours, silly.

MIKE. That would explain the well-rounded individual you are then.

HANNAH. *(laughs flirtatiously)* Oh, stop it.

MIKE. *(laughs flirtatiously)* Wha-at?

ANGELA. Hannah!

HANNAH. Are you still here?

MIKE. So that was it really. It wasn't that I didn't like your jelly beans, or that I was trying to undermine you or what you've done here or anything like that.

HANNAH. Of course not.

MIKE. I can see you've turned it around. It was just the aura in certain departments that left me uneasy.

HANNAH. Angela, I'd like you to exchange positions with Mike. The man is obviously team leader calibre.

ANGELA. But—

HANNAH. Now don't be a sore loser. When a better candidate emerges you have to pass on the baton.

ANGELA. But I thought we were friends.

(No response. ANGELA begins to exit.)

HANNAH. Besides, you bought me a snow globe for Christmas.

ANGELA. You said you liked it.

HANNAH. Well, I didn't want to say anything at the time because you seemed quite happy with yourself. But as a present, it was disappointing.

(ANGELA exits abruptly.)

HANNAH. You're so...I don't know...managerial.

MIKE. And what about my pay?

(Long silence as they stare at each other until finally...)

HANNAH. Yes. Let's talk about that...

(Blackout)

End of Play

Our Prospects For The Coming Season

CHARACTERS

THE MANAGER – male. Wears a suit, possibly Welsh.

THE AGENT – male. Wears a better suit.

THE PROSPECT – male. Wears a tracksuit. From Latin America.

THE PRESS PACK – made of three members. Possibly all female but dressed and behaving as male. Referred to individually as **THE PRESS PACK (1), THE PRESS PACK (2)** and **THE PRESS PACK (3).** When they speak in chorus they will simply be referred to as **THE PRESS PACK.**

OUR PROSPECTS FOR THE COMING SEASON

(Upstage sits **THE PRESS PACK** *lit. Downstage* **THE MANAGER** *stands lit. On the other side of the stage and lit is* **THE AGENT** *standing over* **THE PROSPECT** *who is seated. The rest of the stage is dark.)*

THE MANAGER. Have you seen the boy play?

THE PROSPECT. What are they saying?

THE AGENT. They're asking why they bought you. Just smile.

THE PROSPECT. *(smiling)* Okay.

THE MANAGER. He's a hell of a prospect. The lad's got everything. He's quick, he's as strong as an ox, he's like a human steam train. Two good feet. Right and left. He can open a can of baked beans with that left foot of his. And his right? Like a howitzer. Like he has gunpowder in those boots. He's got good broad shoulders, his thighs are like tree trunks and he has eyes in the back of his head. His vision's fantastic. The boy can pick a pass. He can thread it through the eye of a needle.

THE PRESS PACK (1). And are you looking to play him in the hole linking the midfield with attack?

THE MANAGER. Precisely. Yes. Right from the outset. Behind the lone striker or a front two. Absolutely. Or not necessarily. But that's where he'll end up eventually. I haven't really made a decision. My daughter Susan's been in labour for the last eight hours, she lost the last one the last time at the same stage, so as you can imagine as a family we're all very nervous right now... *(laughs uncomfortably)* ...

(No response. **THE MANAGER** *continues.)*

THE MANAGER. But boy, can the lad dribble though, like a slalom skier, take a man on, it's a lost art but he has that in his locker no doubt. He has a low centre of gravity, see, when he's down there, but up there, in the air, he's unbelievable too, has a phenomenal spring, he leaps like a lizard, like a salmon almost, and he stays up too, soars through the air like a pterodactyl. They're now extinct, but this boy has years ahead of him at the top level.

THE PROSPECT. What's he saying?

THE AGENT. I don't know.

THE MANAGER. He can play out wide, he can tuck in, he can track back, he can hold the ball up top and play with his back to goal. He can head a ball like nobody I've seen. And he's got an old head on those young, broad shoulders too. He can be an influence in the dressing room and a leader on and off the pitch when he learns our English language.

THE AGENT. You're going to be captain.

THE PROSPECT. Great.

THE PRESS PACK (2). And it's a four-year contract?

THE MANAGER. That's right.

*(***THE PROSPECT*** *looks to* ***THE AGENT*** *for translation.)*

THE AGENT. Contract. Four years.

THE PRESS PACK (2). And wages?

THE MANAGER. The figures that have been reported are accurate.

THE PRESS PACK. Four thousand a week.

THE MANAGER. Right.

THE AGENT. *(to* **THE PROSPECT***)* Seven hundred a week.

THE MANAGER. We got him for peanuts really. I'm sure when the sad day comes that he moves on to a bigger club, we'll make a massive profit on the boy.

THE PRESS PACK (3). And how tall is he?

THE MANAGER. How tall is he? *(To* **THE PRESS PACK***)* How tall are you? *(Laughs briefly, and then, unsure, to* **THE AGENT***)* How tall is he?

THE AGENT. How tall are you?

THE PROSPECT. 5'9.

THE AGENT. 5'11.

THE MANAGER. 6'2. He's got a great touch for a big man. His wife's very short but of course opposites attract…

*(***THE PRESS PACK*** laugh politely, perhaps a touch sycophantically.)*

THE PRESS PACK (1). And what about his fitness? He really hasn't had much of a rest close season has he?

THE MANAGER. No, but this lad is a lion. He's like a gazelle really. He has great lungs, plays like he has two hearts sometimes, he can go box to box. He's from a close knit family. He's got a good mother and that's important. Everyone enjoys having a good mother, don't they? Where would we be without the mums? Especially during our births. Doesn't bear thinking about. I think our Suzie would be a wonderful mother. She has a big heart, kind hands…really, she wouldn't say boo to a goose. She deserves it. Life's remarkable, just look at the odds against us before we even get here. It's a mountain to climb just to be born. I'm sure the knockers, the mischief mongers, the doubters, the critics will say I should really be there now. At the hospital, holding her hand, stroking her hair, singing the old songs softly in her ear, kissing her forehead, but football, rubbing her feet, but football, it's like a drug. But when you see a talent like this boy it shows you why you're still in the game. He's streetwise. Doesn't mind rolling his sleeves up. There's obviously going to be a bedding-in period for him early doors, but you only have to look out of the window to see that the whole town is buzzing. And I think we've laid down a marker to the rest of the league. We've really lit the blue touch paper bringing him here.

THE PRESS PACK (3). Are you worried about whether he'll adapt to the fast pace of the English game? At least at first?

THE MANAGER. Well that'll be the acid test of course. But no, I have no worries about him adapting.

THE PRESS PACK (2). Can we ask him a couple of questions about football and life in general?

THE AGENT. Can they ask you a couple of questions?

THE PROSPECT. Yes.

THE AGENT. Go ahead.

THE PRESS PACK. Welcome.

THE AGENT. They're welcoming you. Smile.

THE PROSPECT. *(smiling)* Thank you.

THE PRESS PACK (1). Sorry. What did he say?

THE AGENT. He says it's wonderful to be here. He loves the architecture.

THE PRESS PACK. Awwww.

THE AGENT. Yes, he says it's very different from where he is from.

THE MANAGER. It certainly is. I think on the personal, human aspect of all this, it's great to have taken the boy out of there. We went over in January to watch him play. Of course, it was summer there which was a real mind bender for me and my chief scout. We couldn't quite get our heads around it. But over there the pitches are bumpy, hard and bumpy, it's a wonder they can really play at all. They have some good prospects there, there's no doubt about that, but they just need refining, organization, discipline. But the country itself, deary me, well it only has two seasons for a start. Summer and winter. Dry and wet. And the place stinks to high heaven. It's uncivilized, the people are loud and everything moves at a snail's pace. There are dead dogs lying in the middle of the road, or just about, and everyone seems to live on a bloody great big hillside. The places we saw, golly gosh. I didn't see anyone there with a complete set of teeth. I don't want to get political. I'm a football man. It's in my blood. I'm just saying on a humanitarian level it's been great for the boy to bring him to Milton Keynes.

THE PRESS PACK. Is his family settling in okay?

THE AGENT. Are your family settling in okay?

THE PROSPECT. They're not here yet. It's just me.

THE AGENT. They're not here yet. It's just me.

THE PRESS PACK. That must be difficult for you.

THE AGENT. That must be difficult for you.

THE PROSPECT. Yes…

THE AGENT. I'm a professional.

(A mobile phone rings. It is **THE MANAGER***'s. He takes it out of his pocket without looking at it and turns it off instinctively.)*

THE MANAGER. For now we just have the boy over here. The rest of his clan will be over soon once all the loose ends have been tied up. We pride ourselves on being a family club, it's really part of our make-up and we've really shown great hospitality to the lad. I don't need to remind anybody here that one time, long ago, in a place called Bethlehem, a man and his pregnant wife on a donkey were walking around town, looking for a place to stay, and it looked for all the world as if it wasn't going to be their night, until a kind voice said unto them *"Mi casa es su casa"* and put them in his barn. And I think we all reaped the benefits. There's a parallel here.

THE PRESS PACK. Are you saying he's the Messiah?

THE MANAGER. In a football sense, aye. He can be anything he wants to be. He's the final piece in the jigsaw for our push for promotion and you can quote me on that.

*(***THE PRESS PACK** *are still scribbling in their notepads until…)*

THE PRESS PACK. Does the harsh British winter around the corner give the player any cause for concern given that he is from more tropical climes? Has he enjoyed our August? And how does he feel generally about the changing of the seasons?

THE AGENT. It's very cold here. How do you feel about that? How have you found the weather so far? And all the seasons they have here. Are you looking forward to experiencing more of them?

THE PROSPECT. I think it's very interesting. The different seasons and how one becomes another. There's a lot of great writings and paintings, from great writers and painters that meditate on this theme, but unfortunately I haven't read or seen any of them. There's an old saying in my country that I don't quite remember, but I believe it touches on the subject also...

THE AGENT. It doesn't bother me. I am just a footballer. I'm just raring to go for the new campaign. Come rain or come shine...

THE PROSPECT. We only have two seasons where I'm from. Wet season and dry season. That's really all there is to it. But I love it. And you have four and that's beautiful too. I've liked your August...

THE AGENT. My team mates are fantastic. Even though I cannot speak the language, I can see from their general banter and the way they squirt energy drinks at each other in the dressing room, that they are a great bunch of lads and the team spirit is very good...

(**THE MANAGER** *smiles and nods.* **THE PRESS PACK** *laugh appreciatively.* **THE PROSPECT,** *slightly confused by their reaction, continues regardless.*)

THE PROSPECT. Stretched out, sun cream slathered families. Running races, and giving head starts for those who need them. Tandem bikes and oncoming children, you smile and wave to them as they watch you go. Dancing barefoot, pointing up at the night sky stars, Look there. It looks like a horse. What's that called? You used to know. I don't see it... Oh... Hey, let's go in now. She's beautiful. Something bit me. You love her, and you do, and you do. But these are your borrowed summers. Which maybe you are too quick to return. And now it's September. The autumn fall and the barren winter looms. I'm just a football player, I don't know...

(THE AGENT looks down at THE PROSPECT curiously. THE MANAGER's mobile phone rings. He looks at it and this time decides to take it.)

THE MANAGER. One second. *(Into the phone)* Judy, love. How is she? What's happening?

(He moves out of the light to continue the call.)

THE PRESS PACK. What did he say?

THE AGENT. I've come here to be a champion and prove myself because England is the place to be. I think it's going to be a long hard season. We must have the right attitude and work hard if we are to achieve our objectives.

(Sounds of THE MANAGER sobbing can be heard. THE AGENT is for a moment distracted by this but continues.)

I feel fresh. Everybody has welcomed me with such open arms from the club owner, the coach, down to the canteen staff at the training ground and I want to repay their faith in me with my performances on the pitch.

(Sounds of THE MANAGER still sobbing.)

Thank you for your time.

(THE PRESS PACK applaud and put away their notebooks and get ready to leave. THE MANAGER returns back into his lit area of the stage.)

THE MANAGER. Suzie, she er, there was, er, there was nothing they could do...apparently...nothing they could...do... *(A silence)* ...Do you have any more questions?

THE PRESS PACK. No, that's it. Thank you for your time.

THE MANAGER. Ask me some more questions.

THE PRESS PACK. We have no more questions.

THE MANAGER. ASK ME SOME MORE QUESTIONS!!

(Pause, then blackout on **THE PRESS PACK** *and then on* **THE AGENT** *and* **THE PROSPECT**. *The light gradually fades on* **THE MANAGER** *through the following.)*

Go on...ask me... I...I need questions...

(No response)

My forecast for the season? How I see it. Our prospects.

(No response. The whole stage is dark.)

What about generally? How I see the game has changed over the years.

(No response)

Ask me. *(A beat)* ASK ME!

(No response)

Hello? ... Hello? ... Hell— ...

End of Play

Relinquish

CHARACTERS

YOUNG WOMAN
MOTHER
SON

RELINQUISH

(Lights up on **YOUNG WOMAN** *who takes a notebook from her apron. She approaches* **SON** *and* **MOTHER.** **SON** *and* **MOTHER** *each wear a brown paper bag on their head, with holes cut out for their eyes and mouth.)*

YOUNG WOMAN. Can I get you guys anything?

(No response. **YOUNG WOMAN** *shrugs and exits.)*

SON. I hope you don't feel stupid.

MOTHER. Not at all. Why would I feel stupid?

SON. You have a brown paper bag on your head.

MOTHER. You do too. Do you feel stupid?

SON. A little. But you understand, right?

MOTHER. I think so.

SON. I just want it to be total communication. Not be distracted by faces. No smiling, or crying. Just talking.

MOTHER. Right.

SON. And it was easy to spot you in the crowd.

MOTHER. Likewise. I knew it was you as soon as you walked in.

SON. I hope you didn't get offended that I didn't shake your hand or anything.

MOTHER. No.

SON. And I think a hug would have been a little much.

MOTHER. You're the boss.

SON. Is there anything you want to ask me?

MOTHER. What did you have for breakfast today?

SON. Breakfast?

MOTHER. Yes. I want to know what you eat.

SON. I skipped breakfast. I haven't been able to eat properly since we arranged to meet.

MOTHER. Me neither. Are you glad you're here?

SON. I don't know how I feel. Not really.

MOTHER. I'm interested to know why—

SON. It's been a tough year.

MOTHER. I'm sorry.

SON. My wife left me. I loved her.

MOTHER. It's her loss, I'm sure.

SON. No, it's mine. She's very happy. He's a trampolinist.

MOTHER. Is that a career with prospects?

SON. That's what I asked my wife.

MOTHER. What did she say?

SON. She said that it had its highs and its lows. The joke being that a trampolinist jumps up and down.

MOTHER. Yes.

SON. I would have laughed had I not felt I was dying at the time.

(Silence)

MOTHER. And what is it you do?

SON. I'm a cartographer. Maps.

MOTHER. Right.

(Silence)

MOTHER. I'm a teacher.

SON. I know. That's how I found out you still live here. I was flicking through a programme at a school carnival and saw your name. I knew it was you.

MOTHER. At the school carnival? I was judging the egg and spoon. Were you there?

SON. No. My wife wanted to watch the trampolining.

MOTHER. I heard we won't be doing that event next year.

(Pause)

Do you have future plans?

SON. I'm thinking of going to Vietnam.

MOTHER. My husband's American and was in Vietnam in the early seventies. He didn't like it.

SON. A lot of the country is still unmapped. It's the Tomb of Tutankhamen in cartographical circles. If I like what I see I may settle there.

MOTHER. What was your family like?

SON. My mother was a wonderful woman.

MOTHER. Good. Was?

SON. She's been dead a while. She took a child that wasn't hers and she loved me as if I was her own.

(Pause)

Chalk and cheese.

(Silence)

MOTHER. Do you hate me?

SON. Did you have any more children?

MOTHER. I have two.

SON. You let them stay with you, then?

MOTHER. It was a different time. I was better prepared.

SON. Tell me about them.

MOTHER. Well they're disappointments.

SON. What do they do?

MOTHER. Martin, my next oldest, is a rapist.

SON. Really?

MOTHER. Of women.

SON. Right.

MOTHER. I never raised him to be.

SON. No.

MOTHER. He was convicted and sent to prison last March. Emily, our next—

SON. Nice name.

MOTHER. – thank you – she has the travel bug and fell in love with a rebel fighter from the Congo. She writes occasionally but it's mainly militant rhetoric and her spelling is awful.

(YOUNG WOMAN *enters with two glasses of water with straws.*)

YOUNG WOMAN. I brought you guys some waters.

(*Both* SON *and* MOTHER *hold their hands out and* YOUNG WOMAN *gives a glass to each of them. They sip.* YOUNG WOMAN *exits. No song is heard for the following.*)

MOTHER & SON. *(simultaneously)* Do you know this song?

(*Silence*)

MOTHER. Yes.

SON. Yes. *(A beat)* I love this song and I've never known why.

MOTHER. I sang it to you.

SON. You did?

MOTHER. When I was pregnant and when I saw you last.

SON. I don't believe in that kind of thing.

MOTHER. What kind of thing?

SON. Remembering things from the womb. When you're a baby. That kind of thing.

MOTHER. You were beautiful as a baby.

SON. Was I?

MOTHER. My other two looked like prunes when they came out. But you, you were beautiful. Big blue eyes and pudgy arms. When they cleaned you off, you smelled like heather.

SON. Did I cry?

MOTHER. No, you were quiet.

SON. Not at all?

MOTHER. Only at first.

SON. But I stopped. When did I stop?

MOTHER. You just needed your nose cleaning out that's all.

SON. And then I was quiet?

MOTHER. Peaceful and perfect.

SON. And the nurses, were they nice to you?

MOTHER. Yes. There seemed so many.

SON. And my father?

MOTHER. I haven't seen your father since the first night I met him.

SON. Men are bastards.

MOTHER. Not all men.

SON. Most.

(Pause)

I don't think I'll ever understand you.

(Silence)

MOTHER. No.

SON. But I just wanted to meet you. See what you were like

MOTHER. And how am I?

SON. You're nice. I like your voice.

MOTHER. Thank you. I like yours.

SON. You do?

MOTHER. It's soft. Tender. Like it never wants to be a shout.

SON. Yours is strong. But kind. I imagine that's what makes you a teacher.

MOTHER. Perhaps.

(Silence)

SON. Can I see your face?

(Pause)

MOTHER. You want me to take this off?

(Pause)

SON. Yes. I'd like to see your face.

(MOTHER takes the bag off her head. She straightens her hair. Long pause)

Can I touch it?

MOTHER. What?

SON. Your face. Can I touch your face?

(MOTHER nods. SON moves forward slightly and with an outstretched arm runs his hand over her face. She closes her eyes at his touch. Pause)

SON. You're beautiful…really beautiful.

MOTHER. Thank you.

SON. I never really expected that.

(A beat. YOUNG WOMAN enters.)

YOUNG WOMAN. My supervisor…oh…

MOTHER. What?

YOUNG WOMAN. Well it's just him *(points to SON)* uhm, now. My supervisor wants you to take the bag off your head. It's bothering the other customers.

SON. I was just about to leave.

MOTHER. What?

YOUNG WOMAN. Well I don't mind, it was just my super—

SON. I understand.

YOUNG WOMAN. I'm sorry.

(YOUNG WOMAN exits.)

MOTHER. You're leaving?

SON. Yes.

MOTHER. But we're talking.

(Silence)

MOTHER. Can I see your face?

SON. No.

MOTHER. I showed you mine.

SON. You owed me that at least.

MOTHER. Please. Let me see your face.

SON. Will you tip the waitress?

MOTHER. Yes, but—

SON. I can leave something if you didn't think she deserved it.

MOTHER. No, I'll leave something, but please…

SON. It was good to finally get to see you. It'd been a long time.

(Pause)

MOTHER. Don't go. I want to see your face.

(A beat, then SON *gets up and exits.)*

(Blackout on MOTHER.*)*

End of Play

The Viewing

CHARACTERS

FATHER – ponderous, not indecisive.

MOTHER – enthusiastic, not ditzy.

TOMMY – their adult son. Does not speak in the play. Dependent on parents. Has a learning disability.

ESTATE AGENT – male, with perhaps a trace of the native accent. Wears black rimmed glasses.

SCENE

A backyard outside a property. The weather is very hot. **FATHER** and **MOTHER**, strangers to this foreign land, noticeably feel its heat. The **ESTATE AGENT** does not seem affected by it at all.

AUTHOR'S NOTE

If desired, the play allows for the offstage sounds to be made by members of the cast as an alternative to any sound recording.

When a character shouts it is CAPITALIZED and directed off stage.

THE VIEWING

(Lights up on a bare stage. Sounds of violence and sheer terror can be heard off stage. Orders are being barked in an indistinguishable foreign language. A fearful man shouts back in that same indistinguishable foreign language. There is a gunshot. A woman screams. Another gunshot. A child wails. A third gunshot and then silence. More sounds. Perhaps of flogging or a severe beating being handed out. A single male voice can be heard, but this brutality and the strains of its victim sound further away than the sounds of before and they gradually fade to silence as the **ESTATE AGENT** *followed by* **FATHER** *and* **MOTHER** *enter. They are all dressed impeccably.)*

ESTATE AGENT. *(gestures assuredly to the space before them)* And finally.

FATHER. Oh wow.

ESTATE AGENT. *Voilà.*

MOTHER. We could be very happy here. It's beautiful.

ESTATE AGENT. Isn't it?

MOTHER. Gorgeous. It really is a lovely property.

FATHER. *(points to something)* Oh, look at that. That's wonderful. Really is. *(A beat)* And where's the spring?

ESTATE AGENT. *(pointing)* The spring is located just… there.

MOTHER. What else could you want?

ESTATE AGENT. *(to* **FATHER***)* Gallons upon gallons daily. It's clean too. It's been tested.

MOTHER. Tommy, look at this. *(She looks behind her.)* Where's Tommy? TOMMY!

FATHER. TOMMY! *(A beat)* TOMMY!

(They wait.)

MOTHER. Just leave him.

ESTATE AGENT. Is he alright? He seems rather—

FATHER. He's sulking. Not keen on the prospect of moving. You know how they get. TOMMY! What is he doing back there?

MOTHER. Oh leave him. He's safe. He's just being A GRUMPY LITTLE MONKEY!

FATHER. *(to ESTATE AGENT)* He just doesn't want to leave his friends at home, that's all.

MOTHER. What friends?

FATHER. Darling.

MOTHER. What?

FATHER. Please.

(Silence. Then a blood-chilling scream from a man off stage and another sound of a gunshot.)

FATHER. I really admire the job that you do with such a racket going on. It must get terribly annoying.

MOTHER. Oh, I don't know about that.

(Another sound of a gunshot)

ESTATE AGENT. It's a transitional period here.

MOTHER. I think there's a real passion for life to be heard in all the shouts and screams that go on.

ESTATE AGENT. There is, isn't there? If you listen closely.

MOTHER. The squealing and the wailing. Not to mention the determination and bravery of the removal men which is absolutely terrific to see first hand.

ESTATE AGENT. *(to MOTHER)* Good for you. *(To FATHER)* Your wife is such a positive spirit. I simply can't bear cynicism and there's too much of it these days. But your wife, she's different and I admire that greatly. *(To MOTHER)* I've really warmed to you.

MOTHER. Thank you.

ESTATE AGENT. You're welcome.

(Silence. **ESTATE AGENT** *and* **MOTHER** *look to* **FATHER**.*)*

ESTATE AGENT. *(to* **FATHER***)* You're still not convinced about the property? *(A beat)* Perhaps it's me.

FATHER. No, not at all. You're fantastic. The way you can explain things in such a tantalizing way is an absolute credit to your profession.

ESTATE AGENT. Well, thank you.

FATHER. I must admit…

ESTATE AGENT. What's that?

FATHER. I must admit…I'm really finding it hard to contain my excitement. It's just… If it just wasn't for damn Tommy.

MOTHER. TOMMY! COME OUT HERE, PLEASE!

ESTATE AGENT. He seemed quite captivated by the work of the removal men inside. His eyes were as wide as dinner plates. Is your son's compliance really that necessary to you moving?

MOTHER. Well you know what I think.

FATHER. *(uneasily)* It is, rather. We certainly couldn't move without him. Or against his wishes. I wouldn't really want to do that. Not really.

MOTHER. Weak. You're weak. I've always said this.

ESTATE AGENT. Well, if there's any way we can help you eliminate that obstacle today please let me know.

FATHER. How do you mean?

(Silence. **FATHER** *and* **MOTHER** *look to the* **ESTATE AGENT** *whose look is a little ominous.* **FATHER** *and* **MOTHER** *glance at each other and are visibly uncomfortable with the implication.)*

ESTATE AGENT. *(retreating slightly)* Hey, look. *(A beat)* It is up to you. *(A beat)* There are others interested in the property.

*(***FATHER** *and* **MOTHER** *glance at each other once more.* **FATHER**, *eager to change topic, points to something.)*

FATHER. That will need doing up.

ESTATE AGENT. The previous occupants didn't really do much with it. But of course they're from here and you know what they say about people who are born and live in the same place all their lives.

FATHER. What do they say?

ESTATE AGENT. That they're primitive and have no imagination. I think the person who said "travelling broadens mind" coined that expression too.

MOTHER. Really, that as well? What a clever chap.

(**ESTATE AGENT** *and* **MOTHER** *laugh uproariously.* **FATHER,** *mulling things over, takes out a bag of sweets from his pocket.*)

FATHER. Would you like a Mint Imperial?

ESTATE AGENT. Oh yes, please. *(Takes one)* Oh wait.

FATHER. What?

ESTATE AGENT. Am I—? *(Breathes into his hand and smells)* Does it—?

FATHER. No, I wasn't saying that at all. I just fancied sucking on something. *(To* **MOTHER***)* Mint Imperial?

MOTHER. *(taking one)* Yes, please. Lovely.

(**FATHER** *pops one into his mouth. Silence as they all suck very hard on their mints. After a few moments, they simultaneously take them out of their mouths and toss their mints away in opposite directions.*)

MOTHER. It must also speak volumes for the place that the previous resident's leaving has been so hotly contested by them. In that way they're almost selling it for you.

ESTATE AGENT. I never thought of it like that. *(To* **FATHER***)* She's right. Nobody is skipping merrily out of here. This is a real opportunity.

(**MOTHER** *looks to* **FATHER***. They stare into each other.* **MOTHER** *approaches* **FATHER** *and gives him a tender kiss on the lips.*)

MOTHER. Can we? Please?

(Silence. **MOTHER** *clings to* **FATHER**. *They look a little like newlyweds. Another gunshot is heard from off stage. No reaction from any of the three.)*

MOTHER. You gave a lovely commentary of the interior. Didn't you think so, dear?

FATHER. I'll say.

ESTATE AGENT. Thank you. Needless to say all that will be cleaned up. Everything will be spotless by the time you move in. *(To* **FATHER***)* Sorry. Should you move in. And of course everything will be whitewashed.

*(***FATHER** *and* **MOTHER** *smile at each other.)*

ESTATE AGENT. What is it?

MOTHER. "Transition", "whitewashed". You're so reassuring. You just seem to have a way with words, that's all. It's a scandal.

ESTATE AGENT. *(bashfully)* I used to be a poet. Perhaps that's where it comes from.

MOTHER. Really? A poet?

ESTATE AGENT. No, I didn't really. I don't know why I said that. I used to work at an abattoir.

FATHER. Ah. *(A beat)* Pigs? Chickens?

MOTHER. Sheep?

ESTATE AGENT. Cattle mainly.

MOTHER. Ooh, did you slit their throats?

ESTATE AGENT. *(laughs)* No, I'm far too squeamish for anything like that! I would just walk around prodding them to move along. Their only ever encounter with me in their whole little cow life was me prodding them and telling them to move.

FATHER. And now you're an estate agent.

(Pause)

ESTATE AGENT. *(reciting)*

Consistent cold, damp air.

Rat-a-tat-tat, metal contraptions clatter.

Machinery drones, heavy steel gates slam shut and echo. In for the night.

Strangled calls and cries of a claustrophobic cow.

FATHER. Not bad.

MOTHER. Shit. Lots of shit, I expect? Lots of smell coming from lots of shit?

ESTATE AGENT. I would just view them. Cows can seem such calm creatures. Single file, quiet. They queue like the British. *(A beat)* Except for the one cow at the front of the line who knows what's about to happen. It starts to walk backwards, its legs start to buckle, wobble, it tries to turn around but can't. The space is just too narrow, its body too wide.

FATHER. Blimey.

ESTATE AGENT. And as it struggles, its neck twisting, its front legs kicking, its chin scraping against the side of the chute…you can see. In the one eye that you can see from its side, you can see right into its mind. And it's thinking… *(softly)* "Damn it". *(A beat)* It's too late. Things have gone too far. *(A beat)* And then I would just walk over, prod it and say "move along". And that was it. It had to walk forward. To its end.

(Silence)

FATHER. *(touched)* Poor cow.

MOTHER. *(enthusiastically, misreading the tenor of the moment)* Sounds super! TOMMY!

(**FATHER** *and* **ESTATE AGENT** *look at* **MOTHER** *curiously.*)

FATHER. *(to* **ESTATE AGENT***)* All that wouldn't go down well in India, you know. Cows there are sacred.

MOTHER. *(to* **ESTATE AGENT***)* Oh, they're such a sentimental bunch, aren't they?

ESTATE AGENT. I think your husband is referring to Hinduism. *(To* **FATHER***)* Okay, well. I think that's everything. What's the verdict?

(Pause)

MOTHER. TOMMY! THIS IS YOUR MOTHER SPEAKING, WILL YOU PLEASE GET OUT HERE RIGHT NOW!

(They wait.)

FATHER. TOMMY! THAT WAS YOUR MOTHER SPEAKING AND THIS IS NOW YOUR FATHER. NOW! OUT NOW!

(They wait.)

ESTATE AGENT. COME ON, TOMMY. THERE'S A GOOD BOY.

(Silence. **TOMMY** *enters. His face expressionless, his eyes remain fixed on nothing.)*

Here he is. The main man. How's it going, Tommy? Did you see anything you liked in there?

(No response)

MOTHER. Answer the nice man, Tommy.

(No response)

FATHER. Tommy, we are your parents and we care for you. But you're an adult now and we will not be seen to move against your wishes. But it's a wonderful opportunity and the resources here are fantastic. We want to move here and so we'd appreciate some enthusiasm and support from our son, i.e. you.

(No response)

MOTHER. *(to* **TOMMY***)* The silent treatment. Oh clever. How very clever.

FATHER. Darling.

MOTHER. *(snaps)* What? He has you wrapped around his little finger!

ESTATE AGENT. Perhaps I should leave you alone for a few moments. As a family. *(A beat)* But I do have other appointments.

FATHER. Of course. Would you? We'll be quick, this shouldn't take long.

ESTATE AGENT. Absolutely. I can take a walk, go inside and see what's happening in there.

(ESTATE AGENT *hovers for a moment and exits. Silence.*)

FATHER. I remember a Christmas Day. Do you? *(Pause)* Grandma, my mother, it was to be her last. You had been playing all morning with one of your presents, a new toy, a battleship, from us, I think we said it was Santa who had brought it at the time but no, it was us, we had got it for you. Do you remember?

(No response)

MOTHER. Yes...it was a boat or submarine of some kind. What was it called? There was a cartoon. Could it turn itself into a plane or car too? You loved it. You had wanted it since you saw it advertised in the summer. The batteries were not included.

FATHER. And my gentle mother, she looked so frail, arrived with her gifts, arrived as she did. She handed out her presents. She seemed so excited and pleased with herself and wanted to see your face as you opened yours.

MOTHER. And you unwrapped it and there it was, it was the same toy. She had got you exactly the same boat or submarine as we had given you that morning. And, do you remember what you did? *(A beat)* Do you?

(No response)

FATHER. You hugged her and kissed her like she had just made your world.

MOTHER. You looked so happy.

FATHER. You hid ours so she wouldn't see it and you played with the one she had given you for the rest of the day. And Grandma, my dear mother, she just watched you play. She just watched you all day and smiled. She dropped dead in the kitchen.

MOTHER. Later, that was weeks later, and in her kitchen, but still, it was her last Christmas. It was a lovely thing you did that day. I was so proud of you.

FATHER. Watching her smile like that, it was one of the moments of my life. I don't think I've ever really thanked you for it.

(No response)

Where is that boy now?

MOTHER. That was a beautiful boy, Tommy. The boy who did that.

FATHER. I think we deserve this from you. We deserve your trust, Tommy. Your support.

(No response)

FATHER. Come on, we're pals, aren't we?

(No response. Another blood-chilling scream from a man off stage and another sound of a gunshot.)

You know, somewhere along the line, you turned nasty, Tommy. You were such a beautiful, obedient little boy. But you've grown and changed. And now you're just holding us back. We have to clear every little thing with you. And you know nothing about the way things are. The way the world works. Keeping you informed of every little movement we make. You're...a...a bloody burden. A manipulative, cynical young man who... who...who can't even go to the bathroom by himself!

(Silence. MOTHER appears surprised at FATHER who himself seems almost embarrassed by his outburst. Silence. ESTATE AGENT enters.)

ESTATE AGENT. Everyone's still around. *(A beat)* I really do have to get going. Do we have a decision?

FATHER. I want you to at least indicate to us what your official stance is. What your answer is. You owe us that. Now, please. At least say something.

*(Silence. **MOTHER** appears distraught. **FATHER** watches her for a moment.)*

FATHER. *(to **ESTATE AGENT**)* We're finished here. Tommy would like to go back inside. He needs to get back into the shade, it's too hot for him out here. *(A beat)* Can you please show him inside?

*(**ESTATE AGENT** looks at **FATHER**. **FATHER** nods. **ESTATE AGENT** nods. **FATHER** nods.)*

ESTATE AGENT. Of course. *(A beat)* Come on Tommy. Let's get you back inside, shall we?

*(**ESTATE AGENT** starts herding **TOMMY** slowly offstage. **TOMMY** suddenly start to struggle, trying to break free and trying to turn around, his arms flail, his neck twists, we see the side of his head, he struggles frantically. **ESTATE AGENT** is strong enough to take him off stage.)*

ESTATE AGENT. Come on Tommy.

MOTHER. No...no...

ESTATE AGENT. That's right, Tommy. Move along now. Move along.

MOTHER. *(as she is restrained by **FATHER**)* NO!

*(**TOMMY** is heard shouting off stage. **MOTHER** and **FATHER** grip each other. A sound of a gunshot. A long silence. **MOTHER** and **FATHER** look up and out to the audience as they imagine their future. **ESTATE AGENT** enters. He hangs back and watches the couple.)*

FATHER. This is ours now.

MOTHER. Yes.

(Pause)

FATHER. We'll plant a tree here. For Tommy. Our little soldier. It will be a nice memorial. *(A beat)* For Tommy. And the sacrifice he made.

MOTHER. It'll be our...our Tommy Tree.

FATHER. Yes. *(A beat)* When it grows to a sufficient height, we can lean against it and remember him.

(Silence)

MOTHER. Yes.

(Light fades on **MOTHER** *and* **FATHER.** *)*

End of Play

Frisky & The Panda Man

CHARACTERS

DR OGDEN – male. A slightly anxious panda conservationist.

FRISKY – female. A panda personified. She is the last panda in existence and appears to be a little "under the weather". She still does panda things like pandas do, if a little gingerly.

INTERVIEWER – female. Occupied with her phone or computer tablet throughout. Does not speak.

SCENE

A panda enclosure.

FRISKY & THE PANDA MAN

DR OGDEN. ...well we can all do a little more when it comes to the environment certainly. *(A beat)* But yes, like most people I got into animal conservation for the women. To be frank. At the start. For the ladies mainly. Animals, pandas, well all that came into my focus soon after. They have that effect on you. And Frisky here, well there she is. Just the one panda left. The last peanut in the bowl. She looks, well, "peaky" as you can see. This is how it is now. This is the situation. *(A beat)* Is all of this okay, so far?

INTERVIEWER. . . . . .

DR OGDEN. Anyway, that's a summary. Your hair looks great by the way.

INTERVIEWER. . . . . .

DR OGDEN. I also banged my funny bone on the gate coming in here. I can still feel it now. *(Laughs)* It really hurts! *(A beat)* Anyway, I guess we're not here for small talk. And you've come a long way. This is a big interview, isn't it? A big deal... The End. Yes?

INTERVIEWER. . . . . .

DR OGDEN. If I hadn't been a conservationist? Are you wondering that? Now there's a question. Well, it's funny but between you and me, human to human, and Frisky won't mind hearing this, but underwater photography would have been where I'd have liked to have devoted more of my time. Or any time really. I mean, I haven't ever actually spent a single second doing it. But whenever I've seen pictures of things underwater, and it could be anything at all, fish or old shipwrecks, coral, I always hold my breath and think

"Gosh. Look at that". But that's a whole other world isn't it? Under the ocean, I mean...?

INTERVIEWER. . . . .

*(***DR OGDEN*** watches* **FRISKY** *eat bamboo.)*

DR OGDEN. I do sometimes wonder— sorry? Oh sorry, I thought you said something. Sorry. Yes, I do sometimes wonder if I'd have been happier in my adult life not pandering to pandas like I have. Not spending my days getting them to fuck at least! *(Laughs and then stops)* Sorry, I don't mean to be crude, but that's really been the meat and potatoes of it these last few years. Getting them to have sex. So to speak. Mate. But yes, the seabed. That watery underworld. A secret world. Well it's something else I could have pursued instead certainly. I can imagine myself doing that. Snapping away with my camera. Wearing a snorkel...flippers... it must be so quiet...coming up to the surface, all that ocean spray. That, or maybe something to do with space. The vast solar system. *(A beat)* Do you want me to just keep going?

INTERVIEWER. . . . . .

DR OGDEN. It's not to say I haven't been fulfilled. I've travelled the world. Funny, I always resisted living in London for the longest time. Just thought it was over populated, and I'm not really one for weaving in and out of crowds of people as I'm walking along the pavement. Saying that, when I got the offer from Beijing I was off like a shot. So...well, I don't know... actually, can you just leave that bit out? I may come back to that, it's not very consistent...

INTERVIEWER. . . . . .

DR OGDEN. *(approaching* **FRISKY***)* Yes, it's been an awesome responsibility, I don't mind telling you. *(A beat)* Have you ever been in love? Hurts like hell, doesn't it? Oh well, here's a memory: I won an award and did some lectures some place for a month. Astrid, a woman, came to visit me on my second weekend there. We'd

only been seeing each other every day for three weeks.
It burned so bright between she and I. That first night
of her visit, we made love four, five, six, five, times
through the night, in between we just talked. She made
me laugh and vice versa. It was lovely. It was warm, we
sucked on ice lollies and went through a whole box.
There was a dog. Every now and then we could hear
its footsteps on the ceramic tile and its collar jingling
outside our door. We smoked cigarettes and drank
bottles of beer. We'd get up to brush our teeth together
and come back to bed to kiss again. Neither of us
could sleep because we loved each other so much. We
couldn't believe our luck. She had a beautiful back.
Summer breezes still remind me of her. We later took
a trip across Europe, we went to Genoa, on the coast,
I did most of the driving, all of it in actual fact, she
didn't have a licence. When I opened the car door for
her, she would get in and reach over and unlock my
door as I was walking round. That's when you know
you have a good one and should probably marry her.
She made me see the stars. Life's remarkable. I said to
myself "enjoy this while it lasts". It didn't last. Nothing
does. Genoa. I wish we had our photograph taken.
(Turns back to **INTERVIEWER***)* Sorry, I don't know where
I was — sorry...

INTERVIEWER. . . . . .

DR OGDEN. *(composing himself)* I feel like I'm being
interrogated.

INTERVIEWER. . . . . .

DR OGDEN. Well, yes, anyway, we named her Frisky, but
she's been anything but. We were hopeful that it would
act as an omen, you know? But it's not just her fault.
I mean, the males are as much to blame. To be frank.
Actually the last but one male panda we had here was
called Frank. *(Does not even crack a smile)* Funny. Yes, I
think we were just getting a little tired of the whole
Ling Ling, Chi Chi, Xin Xin naming kind of thing and
wanted to shake things up a bit, but old Frank just took

one look at Frisky here and turned his back to her immediately. "Not if she was the last female panda on earth", which of course she very nearly was at the time and now is. But no, Frank wasn't having any of it. "No way, Jose". Oh, he had a number of health issues and when we finally did get him fighting fit, he died, so... *(A beat)* Yes, but despite the setbacks, my team and I have always made sure that we maintained high spirits about the place. Morale has always been good here. No one around here can be accused of being glum. *Au contraire* there's been plenty of shits and giggles, plenty of *joie de vivre*. I've started using French expressions. I love foreign languages. I wish I could speak one. I had a translator once, he was from Norway and he could speak seven. He was a close friend but he died of a broken heart or pancreatic cancer or some such thing. My translators since haven't really been up to much. He's been a hard act to follow really...

INTERVIEWER. . . . . .

FRISKY. You're avoiding the issue.

DR OGDEN. What?

FRISKY. You are.

DR OGDEN. I'm not.

FRISKY. You are. *(A beat)* Tell her about Max.

DR OGDEN. Max?

FRISKY. Max.

DR OGDEN. *(to* INTERVIEWER*)* Max was the last male panda...

FRISKY. Well, he needn't have been.

DR OGDEN. *(snapping a little)* Will you let me tell the story, please?

*(*FRISKY *goes back to chewing on her bamboo.)*

INTERVIEWER. . . . . .

(Pause)

DR OGDEN. The thing is...well, after Frank. And even before really...well, Frisky's been here for the longest time, haven't you, girl? And well, we got kind of close, didn't we? You'd admit that?

(**FRISKY** *continues nonchalantly chewing on bamboo.*)

Nothing untoward, you understand. Nothing disgusting. Just, when you work alongside someone, with someone, you get, well you get kind of fond of each other. In a way. What with the media events, the photo opportunities, the travelling together, or just here at the enclosure. You bond. Like I said, nothing untoward, nothing disgusting, but I just had these... well, thoughts.

(**FRISKY** *stops chewing on bamboo.*)

Nothing sexual...

(**FRISKY** *continues chewing on bamboo.*)

But just something deeper, you know? Like a connection that transcended everything I'd known before. It was, well, beautiful. It was safe. And I started to see her chastity as a kind of faithfulness to me. Like a form of monogamy, kind of thing. I was very touched by it. Then Frank joined us and well, like I say, he just didn't fancy it, or her, and he passed away. And then it was just me and Frisky again. It was like old times... that was, well, until we got the call from Vienna...

FRISKY. That was about Max probably.

DR OGDEN. Yes.

INTERVIEWER. . . . . .

DR OGDEN. They had someone there. Well, a panda. Called Max. They said he had fucked their last female to death over there. Literally. But they were confident that Frisky was made of stronger stuff and could they send him over, because they were closing anyway. We said *(with some regret)* "sure"...

INTERVIEWER. . . . . .

DR OGDEN. Meantime, while the Austrians were working on all the red tape, the remaining pandas in Asia, Australia, North America, here in Europe, well, the pandas, they were dropping like flies and no one knew why, but we all agreed to keep it quiet for the time being. It became obvious to me that it was down to us here in London to keep the whole panda show going, as it were. We were down to just Max and Frisky. Well I felt torn. I felt nauseous. *(A beat)* So the day arrives and they bring him out and my team took one look at him and they just knew right away. I mean they were high-fiving each other. It was like a space launch. Max, well he just exuded something, you see. It was like you could bet your house on him. And he was...well...let's just say, he was attractive...

(DR OGDEN pours himself a glass of water and downs it.)

I told my team to take the afternoon off. That I'd handle it from here. I think they went bowling. I led Max through that tunnel on your way in here and I just couldn't stop thinking about him having his paws all over Frisky. It made me sick to my stomach. He bounded into the enclosure like he owned the place and well, they both lit up when they saw each other. It was instant, you know. Almost electric or magnetic. Frisky never once looked at me like she looked at Max that day. *(A beat)* Anyway, I just couldn't take it, so I picked up that rifle over there and I shot him.

(Silence)

That shocks you, I expect.

INTERVIEWER. . . . . . .

DR OGDEN. It was a crime of passion really. But I know that doesn't make it alright.

(Longer silence)

My translator was from Denmark not Norway...and he drowned. He was...a good man. *(A beat)* There's a part of me, and I hate this part of me, that's just hell bent on the pursuit. To advance, you know? I'd like to love. I love the concept. I want to love freely but I just can't let things bloom. I can't let it come to me or just occur because what if it won't? I'm insecure. If it's not something to chase, to get, or to control, I'm just not sure I recognize its worth. I just end up destroying things. I'm selfish. *(A beat)* My arm still hurts from that gate coming in. *(A beat)* I don't know, I'm just human, I guess.

INTERVIEWER. *(shaking her electronic device that no longer works)* . . . . .

FRISKY. *(with an orgasmic build)* The sky over Genoa is orange and black. The clouds are purple and green. All in all it's a screaming mess. It's spreading everywhere now. The wind is screeching, birds are flying into each other, planes are falling out of the sky. Everyone's yelling but no one ever listens. The ocean's had enough, it's no longer just a spray, crashing its waves over the tall buildings you built, puking up its underworld all over you all. It's a great spectacle. It's no longer a secret. It's freezing. Everyone's drowning. No souvenir photograph, no dog collar jingle, no translators to help, nothing works now. Any money that anyone ever made, all the conversations in bed anyone ever had, all those laughs, all those whispers, all those promises and kisses, gone, once were, not now, forgotten. It had to stop here. You knew it was coming, you could have done more...That's it really... *(She drops dead.)*

INTERVIEWER. . . . . .

DR OGDEN. Gosh.

(Blackout)

End of Play